The Hercules Story

MC-130E C Rivet Clamp Triple Nickel Ethel of the 8th SOS, pictured at RAF Fairford. (Author)

MC-130H Combat Talon II Night Rider in the 7th SOS, 352nd Special Operations Group, at Mildenhall. (Author)

Fifteen Special Operations Support (SOS) MC-130-1 Combat Talon Is were produced to either -C Rivet Clamp, -S Rivet Swap or -Y Rivet Yank aircraft. Ten MC-130-C 'Clamp' aircraft were fitted with the Fulton STAR recovery system like the one shown. (Lockheed)

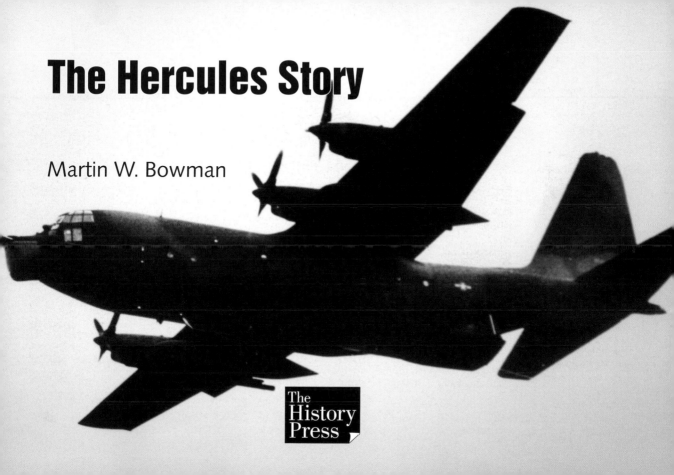

The Hercules Story

Martin W. Bowman

The History Press

Also in this series:

Published in the United Kingdom in 2009 by
The History Press
The Mill · Brimscombe Port · Stroud · Gloucestershire · GL5 2QG

Copyright © Martin W. Bowman, 2009

British Library Cataloguing in Publication Data
A catalogue record for this book is available from the British Library.

Hardback ISBN 978-0-7524-5081-0

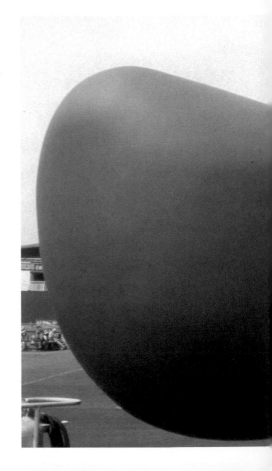

➤
MC-130H Combat Talon II Dawg Pound in the 7th SOS, 352nd Special Operations Group, at Mildenhall. (Author)

Typesetting and origination by The History Press
Printed in Italy

CONTENTS

INTRODUCTION

➤

C-130D Pride of Clifton Park *fitted with skis of the 139th TAS, New York Air Guard. From January 1959 onwards all twelve C-130Ds built were allocated to the USAF Troop Carrier Squadrons.(Author)*

In the years since the Vietnam War, the 'Herky bird' has written its own chapter in aviation history as the world's most successful military airlifter. When military cargo and heavy equipment have to be delivered into trouble zones – soldiers and paratroops, pen-plc, relief supplies and medical aid – or they need to be evacuated from war and famine, then the success of the operation depends on this immensely reliable and versatile craft. When there are labours to be done, whether military support or international relief, the Hercules is usually there, swirling the dust in the middle of desert wastes, being put down on remote jungle strips, or landing on bomb-scarred runways at war-ravaged airports, delivering cargo or air-dropping supplies.

The Hercules has come to the aid of countless thousands in every part of the world. While it can be uncomfortable, especially back in the hold, the rugged, simple construction was designed from the outset to operate from rough or semi-prepared grass or sand strips with the minimum of support.

The Hercules has never been far from the front line. It has continued to prove itself a most flexible workhorse. Since it first took to the skies on 13 August 1954, Herky birds have operated as transporters, gunships, bombers, air-to-air refuellers, airborne command posts, AWACs, firefighters and even airborne hospitals.

Between 1962 and 1975, Lockheed delivered more than 700 Hercules to air forces throughout the world. In April 1994

more than 2,100 models of the Hercules had been sold to over sixty-six countries. When the millennium arrived, the Hercules had been in continuous production for over forty-five years, through at least eighty-five original and modified versions. What about that for versatility! Of one thing we can be certain, and that is that those who are fortunate to have worked with and flown on the Hercules can look back with a deep sense of pride at an airlifter that is without equals.

On 2 February 1951, the USAF issued a request for proposals (RFP) to Boeing, Douglas, Fairchild and Lockheed for a medium-size transport complying with a specially prepared General Operational Requirement (GOR). Experience in Korea, where war had broken out in June 1950, revealed serious operational limitations in the Fairchild C-119 tactical troop and cargo transport. A USAF colonel was reported to have said that what the Air Force really needed was an aircraft that could carry a 30,000lb payload of freight or troops over a distance of 1,500 nautical miles, and could land and take off from difficult terrain. It was a feat, almost impossible to achieve at the time, but sources predicted that the winner of the GOR could ultimately expect to build as many as 2,000 aircraft. The new medium-size transport had to be able to carry ninety-two infantrymen or sixty-four paratroopers over 2,000 miles for tactical missions, or for logistic missions a 30,000lb load (including bulldozers,

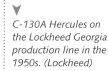

C-130A Hercules on the Lockheed Georgia production line in the 1950s. (Lockheed)

1

2

◄
Line up of the very early production C-130As, the first seven of which were ordered by the Air Force in February 1953.

◄◄
YC-130 prototypes YC-130 53-3396 and 53-3397. The first prototype was used initially for static tests. The second prototype first flew on 23 August 1954.

3

trucks, road-graders and howitzers) over 950 nautical miles (all without refuelling). It had to operate, if required, from short and unprepared airstrips; and it had to be capable of slowing down to 125 knots for paradrops through two side doors, and even more slowly for steep 'assault' landings. It also had to perform with one engine out over the drop zone. At Lockheed-Burbank, Art Flock and his design team, under the

C-130A City of Ardmore, the fiftieth Hercules built, was the first of three in the first delivery to Tactical Airlift Command at Ardmore AFB, Oklahoma, on 9 December 1956.

C-130D 57-0485 Snowshoe, one of a dozen ski-equipped examples conceived in the late 1950s for service in Alaska and Greenland, to support their Distant Early Warning (DEW) line radar stations.

supervision of Willis Hawkins, head of the advanced design department, went to work on temporary design designation L-206. Hawkins said that the new aircraft would have to be an amalgam of jeep, truck and aircraft. Although it was intended as a medium-sized tactical transport, Flock opted for four engines instead of two, which would make the L-206 more expensive than its competitors. No turbine-powered transports had ever been produced in the USA before, but the slim-line 3,750eshp Allison T56-A-1A turbine was selected. The L-206's top speed of 360mph would be faster than any other tactical transport then existing. Its basic mission weight was only 108,000lb due to the widespread use of machined skins with integral stiffening which largely eliminated riveting, and high-strength aluminum alloy was used throughout to strengthen the aircraft's overall structure.

Hercules also featured a 41ft 5in-long cargo compartment of nearly square cross-section for total volume of 4,500 cubic feet.

C-130A 55-0024, which was delivered to TAC in December 1956, carried out a simulated stretcher-borne operation.
This aircraft was then modified in May 1965 to NC-130A Local Yokel for air-to-air missile testing.

C-130B modified to BLC (Boundary Layer Control) test aircraft intended for the proposed C-130C STOL US Army version of the Hercules. Fitted with blown flaps, control surfaces and compressors on the outer wings, it flew for the first time on 8 February 1960.

To achieve ease of loading and unloading, the cargo floor was only 34ft off the ground, or at truck-bed height. The inward-opening top half of the cargo door allowed the Hercules to airdrop equipment and cargo the width of the cargo compartment. In addition

The Royal Australian Air Force was the first overseas customer for the Hercules, buying twelve C-130A examples in 1958. Twelve C-130Es were delivered from 1966. During the Vietnam War the twenty-four aircraft were used between Australia and Vietnam for carrying war material and mail, as well as for medical evacuations. The C-130As were withdrawn from service in 1978 and replaced by twelve C-130H examples.

C-130B of Air Transport Command SAAF, one of seven C-130Bs delivered to South Africa in 1962-63, was allocated to 28 Squadron at Waterkloof, Transvaal, in January 1963.

to a rear ramp, an upward-hinged door was situated on the port side of the fuselage, just aft of the crew entrance door, and there were also paratroop doors on both sides of the rear fuselage, just forward of the ramp. The entire plane had to be pressurized to carry sixty-four paratroops, seventy-eight ground troops or seventy-four litter patients

and two medical attendants (or seventy litters and six attendants) for casevac duties. Above the blunt nose, a spacious flight deck accommodated two pilots, a navigator and a systems manager (a loadmaster made up the fifth member of the crew) in a greenhouse with twenty-three windows designed to give 20° of all-round visibility,

especially during landings at rudimentary airstrips. A strong undercarriage had tandem main landing-gear wheels, which retracted into fairings on the sides of the fuselage. A 132ft-span, high-aspect ratio, angular wing was laid across a flat fuselage and provided excellent ground clearance. The 38ft-high vertical stabilizer was designed to offer easy access to the aft fuselage, and would also permit pilots good control response on low-speed approaches.

The Lockheed proposal was submitted in April 1951 and on 2 July was declared the winner. A contract was awarded for two YC-130 (Model 82) prototype/service-test aircraft, to be built at Burbank, and seven production aircraft (Model 182) to be built at Marietta, Georgia. Al Brown was chosen as C-130 project engineer. The first C-130 prototype (1001/53-3396) was used initially for static tests. The second YC-130 prototype first flew on 23 August 1954, and was airborne within 800ft from the beginning of its take-off roll, and the sixty-one-minute flight to Edwards AFB, in the Mojave Desert, California, was made without hitch. In 1954 orders for sixty-eight more C-130As were received. The

C-130A differed from the YC-130s principally in having provision for two 450 US gallon external fuel tanks outboard of the outer engines, but it was also driven by more powerful T56 engines. The first twenty-seven aircraft were delivered without a nose radome, but were later modified to carry search radar. The first

▲
C-130E of 37 Squadron RAAF at Sydney, Australia, in October 1988. Eight years earlier this aircraft and one other operated Red Cross relief flights to Kampuchea. (Author)

production C-130A-LM (53-3129) was rolled out at Marietta on 10 March 1955. Chief pilot Bud Martin and co-pilot Leo Sullivan flew it on 7 April 1955.

Problems with the reduction-gear system in the Curtiss-Wright, variable-pitch, 15ft, three-bladed propeller units caused severe propeller vibration and were finally

replaced with four-bladed, 13.5ft Hamilton Standard hydraulic propellers. In August 1955 orders were received for eighty-four more Hercules, taking the total to 159, discounting the two prototypes. In June 1956 two C-130As were delivered to the USAF air proving ground command at Eglin AFB for category II and operational suitability tests, which they passed with flying colours. The C-130s also came

Three C-130H aircraft of 401 Squadron of the Japanese Self-Defence Force over their home base of Komaki prior to their deployment to Thimol. (Hayakawa, JASDF)

Svenska Flygvapnet (Swedish Air Force) C-130H firing off ECM flares in a spectacular display. (Peter Liander, Flygvapnet, Stockholm)

18

through gruelling tests in cold climates, and a programme of heavy-lift cargoes and airdrops. Finally, on 9 December 1956, the first operational C-130s for the USAF were delivered, when five were flown from Marietta to the Tactical Air Command's 463rd Troop Carrier Wing, at Ardmore AFB, Oklahoma. First to arrive was 55-0023

City of Ardmore, the fiftieth Hercules built. In September 1958 an order for twelve C-130As with T56-A-11 engines was received for the Royal Australian Air Force (RAAF). It took final C-130A production to 233 (including the two prototypes). In December 1958 a contract was issued for 127 C-130Bs (Model 282) for Tactical Air Command. The C-130B, which first flew on 20 November 1958, differed from the C-130A in that it had an increased internal fuel capacity of 1,820 US gallons, heavier operating weights and was powered by 4,050eshp T56-A-7 engines. Some 230 C-130Bs were built for the US military and a further twenty-nine examples were ordered for the air forces of Canada, Indonesia, Iran, Pakistan and South Africa.

The C-130E (Model 382-4B), which first flew on 15 August 1961, was designed for

◄

C-5 (C-130J-30) ZH889 of the Lyneham Wing flown by Wing Commander Rick Hobson, OC 24 Squadron, on a sortie over the Gloucestershire countryside, going via the Severn Bridge and Weston-super-Mare in September 2001. (Author)

longer-ranged logistic missions. Internal fuel capacity was increased to 6,960 gallons, the two 450-gallon underwing tanks of the earlier version being replaced by 1,360-gallon tanks, re-sited between the engine nacelles. Beginning with the ninth C-130E, the forward cargo-loading door (6.7ft by 6ft) on the port side was dispensed with. Deliveries of the first of 389 C-130Es for Military Airlift Command (MAC) began in April 1962. Argentina, Australia, Brazil, Canada, Iran, Saudi Arabia, Sweden and Turkey ordered ninety-seven C-130Es to take the total C-130E production to 491.

The C-130H-LM (Model 382C) was first delivered to the RNZAF in March 1965. Basically similar to the C-130E, the 'H' is powered by T56-A-15 engines, usually derated from 4,910 to 4,508eshp. They are fitted with an improved braking system and redesigned centre-wing box assembly to extend the service life of the airframe. Sixty-six C-130K-LM (Model 382-19B) Hercules were built for the RAF by Lockheed, with some components coming from Scottish Aviation, and with British electronics, instrumentation and other equipment being installed by Marshall Engineering, Cambridge, before delivery to RAF air support command. The first C-130K flew at Marietta, Georgia, on 19 October 1966, and, as the Hercules C.Mk.1, entered service with 2 OCU at Thorney Island in April 1967. Final deliveries to the RAF of the C.Mk.1 were made in 1968. Thirty C-130Ks were brought up to a standard approaching that of the L-100-30, with the fuselage stretched by 15ft. Some 1,092 C-130H/K models were built. This included 693 C-130Hs for the US armed forces

C-5 (C-130J-30) ZH889 flying via the Severn Bridge and Weston-super-Mare in September 2001. (Author)

Did you know?
The first Hercules entered service in 1956 with the USAF Tactical Air Command.

C-5 (C-130J-30) ZH889 on a sortie over the Gloucestershire countryside, going via the Severn Bridge and Weston-super-Mare in September 2001. (Author)

and forty-six other countries, excluding the UK. USAF versions of the C-130H included fire-suppression foam in the fuel tanks for improved survivability. However, international C-130H versions did not include fire-suppression foam.

USAF and RAF Hercules aircraft were prominent during *Desert Shield*, *Desert Storm* and Operation *Granby* in 1990 during the build up, and throughout the Gulf War, which began on 16 January 1991. More than 145 MAC C-130 Hercules were deployed in support of Desert Shield and *Desert Storm*. These aircraft moved units to forward bases once they had arrived from their respective countries. One of Hercules' first tasks was to move the 82nd Airborne Division from its staging area to positions near the Kuwait border. Throughout the campaign AFRes and

ANG members flew and maintained the aircraft, including those used in strategic and tactical airlift, as well as tanker support, operations. In addition, a small USMC tanker task force was established using KC-130Fs, KC-130Rs, and KC-130Ts and a few USN-operated C-130Fs for logistics support. The EC-130Q was used in the communications relay role. Australia, Great Britain, France, Saudi Arabia, South Korea and New Zealand also sent C-130 transports and KC-130 tankers to the Gulf. By the time the cease-fire came into effect on 3 March, MAC C-130 transports had, since 10 August 1990, flown 46,500 sorties and moved more than 209,000 personnel and 300,000 tons of supplies. They provided logistical support, medical evacuation of the wounded, and battlefield mobility once the fighting started. During the '100-Hour' ground campaign, C-130 transports flew more than 500 sorties a day. More than 2,250 RAF and 550 civil air transport flights had been dispatched, delivering 19.9 million pounds of freight and over 22,800 passengers.

In 1995 a new era began for the Hercules with the appearance of the C-130J (Models 382U/V; designations C-130L and C-130M have never been used). The C-130J/-30 was built to replace C-130s in service with the RAF, the launch customer, and in the US; basically, those with MAC, AFRes and ANG craft. N130JA, the C-130J (RAF Hercules C.4/ZH865) prototype, was rolled out at Lockheed-Marietta on 18 October 1995 and flew for the first time on 5 April 1996.

In 1965 the Viet Cong stepped up its guerrilla war in South Vietnam, and, with the South Vietnamese administration on the point of collapse, the US responded with a continued build-up of military might. Transports were needed in large numbers to support airlift operations, and the Hercules saw widespread service with the USAF, the US Navy, the USMC (as the KC-130F) and the Coast Guard, as well as with the VNAF (Vietnamese Air Force). The RAAF and RNZAF also operated C-130E/Hs on airlift duties to South Vietnam from Australia and New Zealand from 1965 to 1975. The Hercules' main role was aerial transportation. From 1965 to 1972, fifty-five Hercules were lost in South-East Asia alone, and more than half of these in a single year (1967-68). After the spring of 1965 the Hercules became the prime transport aircraft in the Pacific theatre. Its first task, in March 1965, was to airlift troops and equipment to South Vietnam from Okinawa. In May they carried the 173rd Airborne Brigade to South Vietnam in 140 lifts. The US Army considered that air mobile operations using helicopters to deploy troops was a more efficient method than the Air Force paratroop landing method. Then, in August 1965 the 173rd Airborne Brigade was airlifted in 150 Hercules flights. During Operation *New Life-65*, seventy-one C-130s arrived over a thirty-six-hour period to resupply them. C-130s also kept the 1st Cavalry Division supplied for twenty-nine days, delivering, on average, 180 tons of supplies and munitions per day. During spring and summer of 1966 the 1st Brigade, 101st Airborne Division, was transported

Did you know?
More than 2,100 of these much-loved aircraft have been built, and yet the design did not please everyone when it first appeared in 1954. Kelly Johnson, who generated many wonderful sleek designs – the Starfighter and the Blackbird among them – at the Burbank 'Skunk Works', called Hercules 'ugly'.

➤

Paratroops of the 1st Brigade, 101st US Airborne Division, during the airlift from Kontum to Phan Rang, South Vietnam. During the spring and summer of 1966 the brigade was transported on five occasions by the C-130s. Each deployment involved 200 Hercules lifts and each operation was mainly re-supplied by air.

➤➤

Paratroopers in the 101st 'Screaming Eagles' Airborne Division wait prior to being airlifted into action in Vietnam aboard C-130As of the 314th Tactical Combat Wing. (USAF)

on five occasions by the C-130s. Each deployment involved 200 Hercules lifts, and each operation was mainly re-supplied by air. USMC KC-130Fs flew more than 250 lifts into a red dirt strip at Done Ha. Further C-130 flights to the area delivered

large quantities of materials and PSP steel matting. The airstrip was later resurfaced.

The only major US combat parachute assault of the war took place on 22 February 1967, at the start of Operation Junction City, when twenty-two US battalions and four ARVN battalions were airdropped at Tay Ninil and bordering provinces. Thirteen Hercules carried 846 paratroopers of the 173rd Airborne Brigade from Bien Hoa to the drop zone at Katum near the border with Cambodia. Ten C-130s dropped the

during the final stages at the operation, the C-130s carried out airdrops to a 'floating brigade' using drop-zone locations, which the ground unit provided by radio. By the time Junction City finished, 1,700 tons of supplies and munitions had been airdropped by the Hercules. On four other occasions during 1967-68 small teams of US advisers were parachuted in, along with 300 to 500 Vietnamese paratroopers. Each C-130 could carry eighty fully equipped paratroops who were dropped in two forty-man sticks. In November 1967 C-130s lifted the 173rd Airborne Brigade to Dak To in 250 sorties, and they also kept them supplied with more than 5,000 tons of cargo, deposited on the 4,200ft asphalt strip during the three weeks of heavy fighting that ensued.

brigade's equipment, returning in the early afternoon to make further cargo drops. On the next day thirty-eight Hercules flew resupply sorties, and these continued for the next five days, during which daily drops averaged 100 tons. By late March,

Frequently, C-130s parachuted their loads or made use of special delivery techniques.

The remains of one of two Air Force Hercules destroyed on the ground by a Communist rocket attack at Da Nang, South Vietnam, 15 July 1967.

The entire aircraft had to be pressurized to carry sixty-four paratroops, seventy-eight ground troops or seventy-four litter patients and two medical attendants (or seventy litters and six attendants) for casevac duties.

A 317th TAW C-130E performing a Low Altitude Parachute Extraction System (LAPES) delivery of a Sheridan M551 armoured reconnaissance airborne assault vehicle.

➤➤ A TAW C-130E performing a LAPES delivery of a tank. (Lockheed)

There was the Ground Proximity Extraction System (GPES), in which the loads were pulled out of the aft-loading ramp as the aircraft flew a few feet above the ground, by means of a trailing hook which engaged with a cable set up by troops in the field. There was also the Low Altitude Parachute Extraction System (LAPES) in which palletized and shock-proofed loads equipped with large parachutes were simply 'sucked out' from the open hold while the aircraft was flying a few feet from the ground. This method permitted very large items such as tanks and other armored vehicles to be carried, and for them to be deposited accurately to units in the

combat zone. C-130s also made use of the Container Delivery System (CDS), a highly accurate method by which loads could be parachuted from as low as 600ft. Two blind-drop methods, the Adverse Weather Aerial Delivery System (AWADS) which relied heavily on self-contained dual-frequency airborne radar, and another method which relied on the guidance of ground-based radar, were also used.

For three months in 1968 the transports maintained supplies to 6,000 marines at the remote outpost at Khe Sanh, ten miles from the Laotian border and sixteen miles south of the DMZ. The lifting of the Khe Sanh siege was a victory for the Americans and was due almost entirely to this massive air effort. From July 1965 to November 1972 the Hercules flew 708,087 sorties in Vietnam, with peak monthly operations

being recorded in May 1968 when in-country Hercules flew 14,392 sorties. A peace agreement was finally signed on 23

South Vietnamese assist with construction of an airbase in South Vietnam. (USAF)

◄◄
Communist shelling and mortar attacks at Dak To, South Vietnam, on 15 November 1967, destroyed a 1,300-ton ammunition dump and two parked C-130Es. (USAF)

Did you know?
The Hercules was the last aircraft out of Saigon in 1975, jam-packed with, reportedly, 475 people on board with fifty crammed into the flight deck!

Did you know?

In an age when complexity in aircraft design seemed to be the byword, the simple Hercules design consisted of only about 75,000 parts.

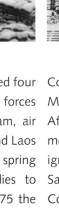

January 1973. All air operations ceased four days later. Although all US ground forces were withdrawn from South Vietnam, air raids into neighbouring Cambodia and Laos continued until August 1973. That spring the C-130s began airlifting supplies to Cambodia. Beginning on 1 April 1975 the wholesale evacuation of all forces left in Vietnam using C-130s of Tactical Airlift Command and C-141As and C-5As of the Military Airlift Command (MAC) began. After 20 April the situation became even more critical and safe operating loads were ignored so transports could take off from Saigon, now completely surrounded by Communist troops, in grossly overloaded conditions. C-130s departed carrying between 180 and even 260 evacuees on board, while a VNAF C-130 is reported to have fled loaded with 452 people. From 1-29 April 1973, 50,493 people had been airlifted during the course of 375 C-130, C-141 and other aircraft sorties. On 30 April Saigon was in Communist hands and the South was under the control of North Vietnam. Six C-130s were among the ninety aircraft flown out of the country to Thailand by VNAF personnel, but about 1,100 aircraft, including twenty-three C-130As, fell into Communist hands before the surrender.

➤

Supplies dropped by C-130s drift towards men of the 1st Cavalry Division (Airmobile) and the 101st Airborne Division in the A Shau valley in April 1968. For nine days, beginning on 26 April, the C-130s flew 165 sorties and dropped 2,300 tons of cargo, most of it ammunition. One Hercules was lost to NVA ground fire and four others received major battle damage. (US Army)

Starting in January 1965, C-130As and crews drawn from the squadrons in Okinawa were attached to the 6315th Operations Group (TAG) control for use as flareships in South-East Asia. Operating from Da Nang, they were used mostly for the interdiction of the Viet Cong infiltration routes through Laos in conjunction with the 'fast movers' (fighter-bombers) such as the F-4 Phantom, in night-strikes against Viet Cong convoys using the Ho Chi Minh trail. Operations in the *Barrel Roll* interdiction area in northern Laos were termed Lamplighter, while those in the *Steel Tiger* and *Tiger Hound* areas of southern Laos were known as *Blind Bat*. Eventually the two operational areas in Laos were merged into one. At peak strength, the *Blind Bat* project numbered six C-130As and twelve crews. The first *Blind Bat* loss occurred on 24 April 1965 (incidentally the first C-130 loss in Vietnam) when it crashed at Karat, Thailand, after the aircraft hit a mountain during a go-around in bad weather. Three more C-130As were lost during the year. In March 1966 the *Blind Bat* project relocated to Ubon, Thailand. Three more *Blind Bat* C-130As were lost in 1968-69. The flare-dropping missions continued until 15 June 1970, when AC-130 hunter-killer gunships, equipped with electronic detection and image-intensifying night observation equipment and a 1.5 million candlepower searchlight, took over.

In 1965 Banish Beach missions were flown by C-130s to deprive the VC of forest sanctuaries by starting forest fires with almost simultaneous drops of fuel drums. Also Commando Scarf bombing missions, in which the C-130s carried small XM-41 anti-personnel mines, were flown, and, in southern Laos, CDU-10 noisemakers were dropped as part of the interdiction campaign. Beginning in 1967 C-130s flew twenty-eight Commando Lava sorties into the A Shau valley, dropping down to 200ft in order to release 120 tons of defoliants so as to deny the NVA and VC forces their entry corridor into South Vietnam. The mud-making operations were no more of a hindrance to the Communists than the annual monsoon and they simply covered over the worst affected parts of the route with gravel or bamboo matting.

In May 1966 the Hercules was employed as a heavy bomber. Operation Carolina Moon was an attempt to destroy the giant 540ft-long, 56ft-wide Ham Rong ('Dragon's Jaw') road and rail bridge over the Song Ma River three miles north of Thanh Hoa in North Vietnam's bloody 'Iron Triangle'

(Haiphong, Hanoi and Thanh Hoa). On the night of 30 May, and again on the night of 31 May, two specially modified C-130E aircraft in the 314th Troop Carrier Wing dropped pancake-shaped bombs, 8ft in diameter, 2.5ft thick and weighing 5,00lb, downstream. When the bombs passed under the *Dragon's Jaw*, sensors in the bombs would detect the metal of the bridge structure and cause them to detonate. In all, ten of the mass-focus weapons were used, but no hits were scored and AA fire shot down one of the C-130Es. The crew were never seen or heard from again. The spans were finally brought down, on 13 May 1972, by laser-guided 'smart' bombs dropped by F-4Ds. By then the Communists had built several other back-up routes around the bridge and so the flow of supplies across the Ma River was not seriously affected.

Countless modifications, such as lengthening the fuselage, have enabled the Hercules to carry large numbers of civil and military cargo, and have resulted in a number of successful variants, including a gunship, bomber, air-to-air refueller, airborne command post, AWACs, fire-fighter and even an airborne hospital.

In 1968-69, under Project *Commando Vault*, C-130s were used to drop 5-ton M-121 bombs to blast out helicopter landing zones in jungle areas, or to demolish enemy vehicle parks and caches. Tests in which a 10,000lb M-121 bomb was dropped from C-130s and CH-54 helicopters proved so successful that late in 1968 the Hercules 'bomber' was assigned to the 463rd Tactical Airlift Wing. In Vietnam, approach to the designated release point was made easier by using signals from the MSQ-77 ground radar sites. The Hercules could carry two palletized weapons in the hold. A single M-121 bomb was capable of clearing an area about 200ft in diameter, and the C-130A/Es could create two clearings per mission, over greater distances than the CH-54. Invariably, bomb delivery was made by the parachute extraction method, usually from about

7,000ft. Stabilizing parachutes were deployed to lower the weapons to the ground. On 23 March 1970 the 15,000lb BLU-82 bomb, capable of clearing an area about 260ft in diameter, was first dropped operationally from a Hercules. 'Big Blue', as it was called, was dropped using a delivery technique similar to that used to unleash the M-120, though a 'daisy cutter' fuse-extending rod ensured that the block-buster detonated at a height of 4ft above the ground. Late in 1971 Commando Vault operations were extended to include troop and vehicle concentrations in South-East Asia. These accounted for many of the 600 weapons dropped (about two-thirds at which were 'Big Blues') in Vietnam, Laos and Cambodia, before the Vietnamese cease-fire in 1973.

In 1991 during Desert Storm, BLU-82B 'Big Blues' were used by MC-130E 'Combat

BLU-82/B 15,000lb 'Big Blue' free-fall bomb (shown without P904 fuse), the 'Mother of all Bombs' dropped by the 7th and 8th SOS teams of the 1st Special Operations Wing MC-130E Combat Talon I to clear Iraqi minefields during the Gulf War. Palletized for carriage in the cargo hold, the bomb was simply jettisoned onto the target. (Author)

Talons', of Special Operations Command, against Iraqi troop concentrations and for mine clearing, with devastating effect. The 15,000lb fuel-air explosive bomb was the largest and heaviest conventional bomb in the USAF inventory. On 15 February 'Combat Talons' began dropping BLU-82 'daisy-cutters' on Iraqi minefields as a prelude to the ground offensive. 'Bombs' containing 16 million leaflets were also dropped by 'Combat Talon' and HG-130N/P aircraft, with messages telling Iraqi soldiers how to surrender to the ground forces. Other 'PSYOP' missions dropped leaflets telling Iraqis that more BLU-82s were on the way.

KC-130F Christine, *the*
Blue Angels' *support*
aircraft, at NAS Whidbey
Island, Washington, in
August 1989. (Author)

C.Mk.1P (C-130K) XV179 coming in to land at Duxford. It was fitted with an in-flight refuelling probe and equipment, as a result of the Falklands War in 1982. (Author)

C.Mk.1P (C-130K) XV292 celebrating twenty-five years of the Hercules in RAF service, at the Mildenhall Air Fête, May 1992. (Author)

◄ *TC-130G* Fat Albert Airlines, *the* Blue Angels' *support aircraft since October 1991.(Author)*

◄◄ *C.Mk.1P (C-130K) XV292 at the Mildenhall Air Fête, May 1992. (Author)*

45

Over the past few decades since 1958 several C-130s, such as MC-130H 85-0012 Combat Talon II of the USAF, have been lost in accidents and conflicts around the world. (Via Ben Jones)

Fourteen C-130Es were modified to the MC-130E 'Combat Talon I' configuration and equipped for use in low-level, deep-penetration tactical missions by the 1st and 8th Special Operations Squadrons, based respectively in the Pacific and North America ('Combat Talons' led the raid on the Son Tay prison camp, twenty miles north-west of Hanoi on 21 November 1970). Largely because of the failed attempt to rescue US hostages in Iran on 24 April 1980, and the subsequent acts of terrorism and hostage-taking, all forces trained in air rescue and special operations were placed under a specialised, unified, USAF command. On 1 March 1983 the 23rd Air Force was activated at Scott AFB, Illinois, with its own helicopters and fixed-wing aircraft. The first test for the new Air Force came on 25 October 1983 during Operation *Urgent Fury*, the rescue of US citizens from Grenada. During the invasion AC-130 gunships and MC-130 and HC-130 tankers played their part very effectively. The operation even had the services of special EC-130E aircraft to broadcast recorded radio programs to the residents of Spice Island. A requirement for airborne radio stations first occurred during the Dominican Crisis of 1955 when it was found that broadcasting capability was needed to break into civilian and military radio networks. In 1977 the 'Persuaders in the Sky' took delivery of their first EC-130E, and they became an all EC-130E force in March 1979. In December 1989 and January 1990 *Coronet Solo* EC-130Es were used during Operation *Just Cause*, the US invasion of Panama, to broadcast misinformation to Panamanian forces. Three MC-130E 'Combat Talons' helped secure the airfield at Rio Hato AB, under fire, with two HC-130 refuelling tankers supporting them. MC-130E 'Combat Talons' and MH-53E helicopters were used to carry US Navy SEALS (Sea-Air-Land) infiltrating Panamanian positions. This was the 23rd Air Force's final operation before its deactivation.

On 22 May 1990 the 23rd Air Force became a USAF component of the Air Force Special Operations Command (AFSOC), when Special Forces of each branch of the armed forces came under central operational control at Hurlburt Field, Florida. No less than fourteen special operations squadrons, plus two AFRes units, operate throughout the US, the Pacific and

C.Mk.1P XV306 The Baron displays the first piece of RAF Gulf nose art. Several of the Lyneham Wing Hercs received nose art during the conflict. (Author)

Europe. AFSOC organises trains, equips and educates Air Force special operations forces, and missions include air traffic control for establishing air-assault landing zones, close air support for strike aircraft and AC-130 'Spectre' gunship missions, establishing casualty collection stations and providing trauma care for injured personnel.

Deliveries of twenty-four MC-130H 'Combat Talon II' aircraft, the first of which

flew in 1988, began in mid-1991. These aircraft are fitted with an in-flight refuelling receptacle, have explosion-suppressive fuel tanks, a modified cargo ramp area for high-speed, low-level aerial delivery, Emerson Electric AN/APQ-170 precision terrain-following and terrain-avoidance radar, dual radar altimeters, dual INS and, finally, provision for a CPS receiver. Some twenty-eight MC-130P 'Combat Shadow'/

50

tanker aircraft are in service with AFSOC for single-ship or formation in-flight refueling of its *Pave Low* special operations helicopters working in a no- to low-threat environment.

On 7 January 1991 the Joint Task Force (JTF) was activated at Ramstein AB, Germany, and one of its components, the Special Operations Task Force, was to seek and rescue downed Allied pilots. On 17 January three EC-130s were among the European units that deployed to Incirlik AB, Turkey. Six MC-130E 'Combat Talon Is', were deployed to Saudi Arabia for Operation *Desert Storm* missions in the Gulf War, which began on 16 January. EC-130Es helped to psychologically prepare the battlefield for Desert Storm, being among the first aircraft to be sent to the Gulf region. On 22 November the unit began PSYOP operations, broadcasting the 'Voice of America' into Iraq, Kuwait and Saudi Arabia. A crash modifications program, lasting several weeks, upgraded the EC-130Es so that the *Commando Solo* aircraft could broadcast in the local TV format for this region. Leaflet drops and broadcast readings from the Koran, as well as testimonials from Iraqi prisoners, were instrumental in persuading Iraqi troops to surrender. When surveyed, Iraqi PoWs indicated that PSYOP radio broadcasts reached fifty-eight per cent of the military target audience. Of those, forty-six per cent indicated that the broadcasts had an influence on their decision to surrender.

C.Mk.1P (C-130K) XV297 unloading light tanks. (Author)

AC-130 gunships have evolved since November 1965, when 'Spooky' AC-47 gunships were used in Vietnam. The AC-47s demonstrated such highly effective convoy escort and armed reconnaissance over the Ho Chi Minh Trail that in June 1967 flight-testing of a JC-130A modified to Gunship II/'Plain Jane' configuration began. It was fitted with four portside-firing General Electric MXU-470 7.62mm GAU-2 miniguns and M-61 20mm Vulcan cannon to fire obliquely downward. Vulcan

AC-130A gunship firing one of its two 40mm Bofors cannon. The AC-130A and E versions were armed with two 20mm cannon, two 7.62mm miniguns and two 40mm Bofors cannon, ranged along the port side of the fuselage and slaved to fire-control radar and a range of sophisticated sensors. (Lockheed)

Express, as the Gunship II was named, was also equipped with a Starlight Image-Intensifying Night-Observation Scope, side-looking radar, computerised fire-control system, beacon tracker, DF homing instrumentation, FM radio transceiver and an inert tank system. A semi-automatic flare dispenser and a steerable 1.5 million candlepower searchlight containing two Xenon arc lights (infra-red and ultra-violet), were mounted on the aft ramp. The Gunship II was dispatched to Nha Trang, South

Vietnam, in September 1967 for combat evaluation. Though the complexity of its sophisticated equipment was responsible for many scrubbed missions, Vulcan Express acquitted itself well, and in 1968 received additional evaluation along the Ho Chi Minh Trail.

Project Gunboat, as it was code-named, went so well that seven more JC-130As were converted to the AC-130A gunship configuration, and were delivered in 1968. These differed from the prototype in having improved systems, including side-looking infra-red and Moving Target Indicator

(MTI) sensors and an analog computer. On 31 October 1968, the 16th SOS at Ubon – call sign 'Spectre' – were activated, and the *First Lady* became its first AC-130A gunship, used initially for night interdiction and armed reconnaissance missions during *Barrel Roll* operations in Laos. Ubon became the home of the AC-130 gunships for the rest of the war; being used to mount operations in Cambodia until shortly before the cease-fire came into effect on 15 August 1973. The AC-130 gunships were used very effectively at night, mainly on out-country operations and, in particular, on the Ho Chi Minh Trail on *Commando Hunt* interdiction missions. All-weather operation and larger-calibre gun requirements meant the AC-130As were modified to *Pave Pronto* configuration under the *Super Chicken*, or *Surprise Package*, program. They wreaked havoc among enemy convoys at night, and used their laser designator/rangefinder to mark targets for F-4D Phantoms carrying Laser-Guided Bombs (LGBs). Two AC-130As were lost on operations.

In 1970 two AC-130E prototype gunships were built using C-130E airframes whose higher gross weight, stronger airframe and

The *First Lady* motif on the forward fuselage of AC-130A 53-3129. *(Author)*

The 25mm GAU-12/U cannon, which is belt fed with 3,000 rounds of ammunition, used on the AC-130U Spectre gunship. This gun replaced the twin GE M61 20mm cannon arrangement used on all previous AC-130 gunships. (Author)

increased power offered a greater payload and longer periods of loitering. More advanced avionics were fitted and the 'Pave Aegis' armament configuration was created by installing a 105mm howitzer in place of one of the 40mm cannon in the port parachute door, while retaining the two 20mm cannon forward of the port undercarriage fairing. The howitzer was later attached to a trainable mounting controlled by beacon-tracking radar. Nine more C-130E conversions followed. By the summer of 1971 they became known as 'Pave Spectre Is', the first entering combat in the spring of 1972 when they helped repulse the Viet Cong offensive. AC-130Es proved most effective tank killers during night operations and on night interdiction sorties along the notorious Ho Chi Minh Trail. All the AC-130Es, except one which was shot down in March 1972, were upgraded in June 1973 to AC-130H standard, being re-engined with 156-A-15 turboprops. Also, the 7.62 miniguns were omitted.

In December 1989 and January 1990, during Operation *Just Cause*, the US invasion of Panama, Hercules gunships were among the first in action early on the morning of 20 December, destroying the Panamanian Defense Force's Comandancia HQ with devastating fusillades of cannon and machine-gun fire. In 1990 the AFRes deployed some AC-130As to Turkey for Operation *Proven Force*, the 'second front' for the coming war with Iraq. Eight AC-130H gunships were deployed to Saudi Arabia for Operation *Desert Storm* missions. While defending a USMC force under attack by Iraqi forces on 31 January, an

AC-130H was shot down sixty-eight miles south-south-east of Kuwait City, with the loss of all fourteen crew.

In Somalia, in June-July 1993, when American air units fought to prevent

AC-130U 90-0167 Spectre gunship, one of thirteen based on the C-130H airframe modified by Rockwell International. (Author)

➤
AC-130H Hercules gunship. The AC-130E and -H retained the 'Black Crow' ignition detector, while the E retained the twin 40mm Bofors cannon; but as this dramatic photograph shows, the AC-130H introduced a 105mm howitzer in place of the two cannon. (Lockheed)

General Aideed and his supporters retaking control of Mogadishu, AC-130H gunships and Cobra helicopters of a US Army quick-reaction force were used in day and night actions against the terrorists. In a one-hour attack, on 11/12 June, the 'Spectre' gunships and Cobra helicopters destroyed Aideed's radio station while American soldiers led attacks on his command headquarters and weapons caches. On 14 March 1994 an AC-130R Spectre crashed in the sea after take-off from Mombassa, Kenya, when a howitzer round exploded in the gun-tube and caused a fire in the left-hand engines. Eight crewmembers died. Three of the six survivors stayed with the aircraft during the crash-landing, while the other three parachuted to safety. That same year delivery of AC-130U Spectre gunships began. These resulted from a July 1987 decision to replace the AC-130As, and thirteen new C-130H airframes were procured for the modification. These carried the same armament as the AC-130H, except that the trainable GAU-12/U 25mm Gatling gun replaced the two 20mm cannons. All weapons can be slaved to Forward-Looking Infra-Red (FLIR) digital fire control radars, mounted under the port side of the nose, or turret-mounted All-Light Level TV (ALLTV) in the port main undercarriage, for true adverse weather ground-attack operations. The 'Black Crow' truck ignition sensor, radome and separate beacon-tracking radar used on earlier gunships were omitted. Observer stations were included on the rear ramp and starboard forward fuselage side. A whole host of other equipment, including a Global Positioning System (GPS) and

AC-130U gunship Bad Company. *(Author)*

Spectra ceramic armour protection, under-fuselage chaff and flare dispensers, FLIR countermeasures and jammer were fitted to increase survivability in a low-to-medium-threat environment. The eighteen 'U-boats', as they are known, also provide escort, surveillance and reconnaissance/ interdiction and other special operational roles, in addition to the primary precision fire support mission.

The Hercules' humanitarian role may account for the great affection which the C-130 seems to inspire. Throughout the 1970s and '80s RAF C-130s assisted in earthquake, typhoon and cyclone relief operations, and delivered thousands of tons of rice and maize to starving peoples in famine-inflicted areas around the world. Then, in 1982, the RAF C-130 fleet was called upon for its greatest challenge so far. On 2 April Argentinean forces invaded the Falkland Islands, and the

◀
C-130H of the Belgian Air Force, one of twelve delivered to Belgium between June 1972 and 1973. They have been widely used in humanitarian and relief roles for the United Nations. (Lockheed)

61

◄◄
DC-130A of Fleet Composite Squadron -3 (VC-3) armed with three BOM-34 Firebee target drones in August 1975. (USN)

◄
WC-130B 62-3495, one of five weather reconnaissance versions produced in 1962 for the air weather service by Lockheed. That same year they entered service with the 55th Weather Reconnaissance Squadron at Ramey AFB, Puerto Rico, where they were used on hurricane- and typhoon-hunting missions in the region. This aircraft was acquired by the Tunisian Air Force in January 1998. (Author)

British Government mounted Operation *Corporate* to retake the islands. On 21 April, the first airdrop by Hercules from Ascension Island (4,260 miles from Britain and 3,915 miles from Port Stanley) to ships of the task force took place. In the first three weeks of Operation Corporate Hercules aircraft made 163 flights and

The Crown, a JATO-equipped LC-130F of VX-6, blasts off from a snowfield in Antarctica. This aircraft was delivered to the US Navy in August 1960, and made its first flight into the Antarctic in the winter of 1962.

An RAF Hercules comes in to land at RAF Port Stanley after the Argentinean surrender ended the Falklands War in 1982. Abandoned Fuerza Aérea Argentina Pucaras litter the side of the runway. During the conflict the Fuerza Aérea operated one of its C-130Hs as a bomber, making a British ship the target for a salvo of eight bombs. One of the bombs hit the ship but, fortunately, failed to explode, bouncing off into the sea. A week later a US-leased oil tanker, coincidentally named Hercules, on its way round Cape Horn in ballast, was also hit, but again the bomb failed to explode and the weapon finished up lodged below decks. The ship eventually had to be scuttled.

On 18 June 1982, Flight Lieutenant Terry Locke and his crew in 70 Squadron set a new world duration record for the Hercules in C.Mk.1P XV179, on an airdrop mission to East Falkland lasting twenty-eight hours and four minutes.

XV200, the prototype RAF C.Mk.1P, made its first flight after being fitted with a fuel probe on 28 April 1982. On 5 May this Hercules successfully transferred fuel to a Victor K.2. A new air-to-air refuelling 'toboggan' technique was adopted because of the disparity in speeds between the Victor and the Hercules, which meant that the Victor had to approach the Hercules from above and astern. The Victor then had to overtake, slowly, allowing the Hercules to move into the 6 o'clock position to engage the drogue and continue the descent at about 500ft per minute for fifteen minutes, at a speed of 270mph. XV200 reached Widewake on 12 May, and the first Hercules' air-refueled, long-range airdrop sortie to the Total Exclusion Zone (TEZ), imposed by British Forces around the Falklands, went ahead on 16 May. (Marshalls)

C-130H of the Canadian Armed Forces during a JATO rocket-assisted take-off. This Hercules was lost in a mid-air collision with another CAF C-130H over CFB Namao on 29 March 1985. (Lockheed)

C-130E 10320, which was delivered to the RCAF (Royal Canadian Air Force) in August 1965. Fourteen C-130H aircraft were diverted to the RCAF from the USAF Tactical Air Force allocations between October 1974 and February 1991. (Lockheed)

C-130E of the Turk Hava Kuvvetleri, one of eight delivered to the Turkish Air Force under the US Military Assistance Program (MAP) in 1964. (Turkish Air Force)

➤➤
C-130H B-679, one of three delivered to the Royal Danish Air Force between April and July 1975. (Lockheed)

delivered almost 1,500 tons of stores and equipment for the task force. However, C-130K range restrictions required immediate provision for in-flight refuelling, and surplus 825 imperial gallon auxiliary tanks were installed in the forward fuselage of the C.Mk.1s, thus increasing their range by approximately 1,000 miles and extending the maximum endurance by about four hours. Installing four tanks in the forward fuselage, instead of two, affected a further increase in range, and the first of these versions was deployed to Ascension on 4 May. Meanwhile, Marshall Engineering of Cambridge urgently installed, tested and fitted in-flight refuelling probes to twenty-five C.Mk.ls, and went on to convert another six to serve as tankers. Problems during trial 'prods' with Victor K.2s were gradually eliminated, and the first of the Hercules' air-refuelled, long-range, airdrop sorties to the Total Exclusion Zone (TEZ), imposed by British Forces around the Falklands, went ahead on 16 May.

On 3 June 1982 the RAF recorded its 10,000th hour of Hercules operations since Corporate began. In fourteen weeks of operation Ascension handled over 18,000 tons of freight and 42,000 passengers, all without loss. The contribution made by the Hercules fleet in the Falklands War was immense. Many lessons were learnt, and, beginning in 1986, Marshall began fitting in-flight refuelling probes to the thirty C.Mk.3s to convert them to the C.Mk.3P configuration. Starting in 1987, C.Mk.1.Ps and C.Mk.1.Ks began receiving jamming equipment and chaff/flare dispensers. At least five C.Mk.lPs were fitted with 'Orange Blossom' ESM pods beneath their wing

C-130D of the 139th TAS, New York ANG, taxiing near an Early Warning Radar outpost of the Dye Line in Greenland in the late 1970s.

tips, to give some degree of surveillance capability.

In July 1991 the plight of the Kurds of Northern Iraq, following their failure to overthrow Saddam Hussein, resulted in the US-led *Provide Comfort* relief operation for the UN *Safe Haven*. On 7 April USAF aircraft began dropping food, blankets, clothing, tents and other equipment to the Kurdish refugees. Eventually, thirteen countries took part in *Provide Comfort*, and another thirty were to provide various types of material assistance. By 8 April USAF aircraft had dropped approximately 27 tons of relief supplies to the Kurds. On 9 April the mission expanded to sustaining the refugee population for thirty days. Two days later *Provide Comfort* took on the additional responsibility of providing temporary settlements for the Kurds. By

6 June the last mountain gap had closed and the refugee population was in the security zone, or 'safe haven'. *Provide Comfort* ended on 15 July, and the emphasis then shifted to preventing a recurrence, with Operation Provide Comfort II.

In April 1992 USAFE C-130Es at Rhein-Main AFB, five miles south of Frankfurt, took part in Operation *Provide Hope II*, a long-term effort to aid cities in the former Soviet Union. On 4 and 5 May a US European command joint special operations task force rescued

HC-130H (crown bird) rescue and recovery aircraft of the 67th ARRS (Aerospace Rescue and Recovery Squadron). The first HC-130H was delivered on 26 July 1965, and all were equipped with the nose-mounted Fulton STAR (Surface-To-Air Recovery) personnel recovery yoke.

RAF W.Mk.2 (C-130K) XV208, which was delivered in September 1967, was, in 1972, converted into a flying testbed for the meteorological flights of the RAE at Farnborough. (Author)

Nepalese children at Surkhet sift grain just brought to them by C.Mk.1 XV200 of No.40 Group RAF Transport Command during the March 1973 Operation Khana Crusade, the biggest airlift since Berlin in 1948, in which Hercules dropped almost 2,000 tons of grain, maize and rice to Himalayan villagers in Nepal. In 1980 the RAF Hercules returned, in Operation Khana Cascade. Also, in 1973 Hercules assisted in famine relief in Sudan, Mali, and West Africa, and deployed UN peacekeepers to the Middle East after the Yom Kippur War.

The W.Mk.2's 26ft (7.9m) long proboscis painted with red and white stripes had a laser projector and camera to take three-dimensional pictures of cloud samples. (Author)

438 people from Freetown, Sierra Leone. From 12 August to 9 October three C-130Es were deployed from Rhein-Main to Luanda, Angola, to be used to relocate government and rebel soldiers during Operation *Provide* *Transition*, a multi-national UN effort to support democratic elections following the civil war in Angola. The C-130s flew 326 sorties, carrying 8,805 passengers and 265 tons of cargo during the operation. On 3 July 1992 the first two C-130s took part in the first *Provide Promise* mission, laden with humanitarian relief supplies for war-torn Sarajevo. Operation *Cheshire* began in the summer of 1992 when a RAF Hercules

➤➤
Lockheed modified XV223 as the prototype of the Hercules C.Mk.3, with its fuselage 'stretched' by 15ft (4.57m) to increase capacity from ninety-two to 129 infantrymen, or from sixty-four to ninety-two paratroops. This aircraft first flew in modified form on 3 December 1979. Twenty-nine C.Mk.Is (including XV217) were subsequently stretched by Marshall Engineering to bring them up to C.Mk.3 standard. (Lockheed)

➤
The Forca Aérea Portugesa acquired five C-130H aircraft in 1977-78, the third of which was 6803, delivered in April 1978. (Aviation Workshop)

➤
The Al Quwwat Almalakiya (Royal Jordanian Air Force) acquired four ex-USAF C-130Bs in 1973, followed by four C-130Hs in 1978. (Author)

began flying into Sarajevo three times a day.
As at the end of October 1993, the RAF had
delivered 12,500 tons of aid to Sarajevo in
880 visits, and flown close to 2,000 hours
in the process. The last relief flight into
Sarajevo was on 9 January 1996. Overall,
the UN effort totaled 160,370 tons of aid,
and included flights from the air forces of
Canada, the US, Germany and France. In

◄

Captain Paul Britton of the 773rd ALS, 463rd TAW, piloting a C-130H, skirts the Somali terrain on an Absolution mission to Mogadishu on 1 March 1993. (Author)

March 1993 the US operation expanded to include the airdrop of relief supplies to Bosnia-Herzegovina. On 27 February a USAF Hercules first dropped about a million leaflets in less than forty minutes over eastern Bosnia, telling residents and refugees that airdropped relief was on its way, and cautioning people of the dangers of being too close to the drop zone. Night after night Bosnian refugees stood in the open, and waited for the 'parcels from God' to drop.

➤ *Welcome to Mogue! Captain Paul Britton of the 773rd ALS, 463rd TAW, on the top of his C-130H during an Absolution mission to Mogadishu on 1 March 1993. (Author)*

➤ *C.1P XV185 and C.1P XV293, the two RAF Hercules used in Operation Vigour, at Moi International Airport, Mombassa, Kenya, on 28 February 1993, the day before they returned home to RAF Lyneham. (Author)*

C-130E of the 711th SOS, 919th SOG, from Duke Field, Florida (note the skull & crossbones above the doorway), and a C-130H (behind) of the 722nd ALS, 463rd TAW, from Dyess AFB, Abilene, Texas, at Moi International Airport for Operation Provide Relief in February 1993. (Author)

In August 1992 heavily armed, organised gangs were stealing food and famine relief supplies from humanitarian organisations in the famine-ravaged East African state of Somalia, so ten C-130s and 400 personnel were deployed to Moi International Airport, Mombassa, in Operation Provide Relief. This multi-nation air operation also involved

Cockpit of an HC-130H of the US Coast Guard. (Author)

➤
HC-130H and EC-130V of the US Coast Guard at CGS Clearwater, Florida, in March 1998. The EC-130V is an HC-130H modified to an early-warning aircraft, with a rotordome (radar AN/APS-125) and an AN/APAS-14S, and was delivered to the USCG in May 1988. (Author)

➤
HC-130H of the US Coast Guard at CGS Clearwater, Florida, in March 1998. (Author)

HC-130H of the US
Coast Guard coming in to
land at CGS Clearwater,
Florida, in March 1998.
This aircraft was one
of eleven HC-130H-7
aircraft delivered to the
USCG between 1985 and
1987. (Author)

Did you know?
N130JA, the C-130J
(RAF Hercules C.4/
ZH865) prototype,
was rolled out at
Lockheed-Marietta on
18 October 1995, and
flew for the first time
on 5 April 1996.

Great Britain, Germany, France, Italy, Belgium and Canada, under the leadership of the United Nations in Nairobi. Provide Relief continued until the end of February 1993, by which time the multi-national unit had flown 1,924 sorties to Somalia and 508 to Kenya, and had carried over 28,000 tons of food for the international relief effort. The C-130s operated from austere, dusty runways as short as 3,000ft, and sometimes littered with rocks, but without a single accident or mission failure due to maintenance problems.

◄

HC-130H, one of a batch of twenty-four for the US Coast Guard, was delivered to Clearwater, Florida, in December 1986. (Lockheed)

◄

Fifteen HC-130N aircraft (69-5826 pictured) were produced for the air force rescue service in the 1970s. The HC-130Ns were re-designated MC-130Ps in January 1998. The MC-130P's primary role is to conduct single-ship or formation in-flight refuelling of special operations forces' helicopters in a low- to selected medium-threat environment. (Author)

◄

*USAF C-130s
at Mombassa,
Kenya, during the
international relief
operation to the
famine-inflicted
East African state
of Somalia in 1993.
(Author)*

◄◄

*N1130E, the L-100
demonstrator, which
first flew on 20/21
April 1964, at a remote
African airstrip during
testing. The aircraft was
later 'stretched' and
modified to L-100-20
standard.(Lockheed)*

▲

*A Swedish Air Force
Hercules at Moi
International Airport,
Mombassa, Kenya, during
the international relief
operation to Somalia in
1993. (Author)*

▶

SAFAIR (Southern Air Transport, based in Miami, Florida) L-100-20 and L-100-30 Hercules at Moi International Airport, Mombassa, Kenya, during the international relief operation to the famine-inflicted East African state of Somalia in 1993. (Author)

▶

Captains Mike P. Brignola (centre, right) and Darren A. Maturi (right, hands behind back) brief their 41st ALS, 43rd ALW, crew in front of C-130E 64-0529 at Rhein-Main before the 'off' for the night airdrop at Bjelimici, Bosnia, on 24/25 March 1994. (Author)

Last-minute instructions from Captain Mike P. Brignola (right) to Darren A. Maturi's crew (to Brignola's right) at Rhein-Main before the night airdrop at Bjelimici, Bosnia, on 24/25 March 1994. (Author)

Captain Mike Brignola goes through the pre-flight check with Captain Darren Maturi. (Author)

91

► MREs (Meals Ready to Eat) in the rear cargo hold of a USAF C-130. The Tri-Wall Aerial Delivery System (TRIADS) was first used in March 1993 over Srebrenica. In this method individual HDR packets packed into cardboard boxes are 'fluttered' onto DZs. The boxes have walls made of three layers of cardboard and self-destruct after leaving the C-130. The individual HDRs then scatter and fall to the ground in much the same way as a leaflet drop. (USAF)

MREs leaving the rear cargo hold of a USAF C-130 over Bosnia. On the night of 23/24 August 1993 USAFE C-130s flew over Mordar and discharged, in a 'free-fall', 13,440 individual MRE packs weighing about 20lb (9kg) each, in boxes designed to open in mid-air, spreading the packages over a wide area. (USAF)

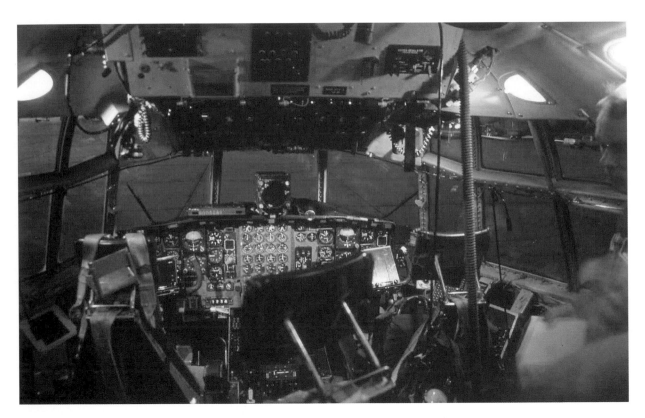

C-130E of the Turk Hava Kuvvetleri at the 1998 Mildenhall Air Fête. This aircraft was delivered to the Turkish Air Force under the US Military Assistance Program (MAP) in October 1964. (Author)

C-130H 91-1231 of the 165th ALS, Kentucky Air National Guard (ANG), the 2,000th Hercules built which was delivered to the 165th in May 1992. This was the first aircraft with SATIN (a missile warner; chaff and flare dispenser).(Author)

C-130E cockpit. (Author)

A C-130E Hercules of 37 Squadron RAAF at Dili airfield unloads medical equipment following the Indonesian military atrocities, not long after the independence referendum of September 1999. (Australian Defence HQ)

C-130E of the 96th TAS, 934th AG, AFRes piloted by 1st Lieutenant Ross Becker, en route to Sarajevo from Rhein-Main, on 23 March 1994. Staff Sergeant Ronald A. Downer, the flight engineer, checks his calculations. (Author)

Did you know?

In 1965 an order for sixty-six C-I30Ks was placed by the British Government, making the RAF the second-largest Hercules user after the USAF.

C-130E of the 96th TAS, 934th AG, AFRes, piloted by 1st Lieutenant Ross Becker, crossing the Alps en route to Sarajevo on 23 March 1994. (Author)

1st Lieutenant Eric L. Meyers checks his Provide Promise notes.

1st Lieutenant Ross Becker at the controls of C-130E over Bosnia (note the flak jacket) on 23 March 1994. (Author)

97

C-130E of the 96th TAS, 934th AG, AFRes, piloted by 1st Lieutenant Ross Becker and 1st Lieutenant Eric L. Meyers, on its final approach to Sarajevo, 23 March 1994. (Author)

Welcome to Sarajevo! (Author)

In 1959 Lockheed announced that Pan American Airways had ordered twelve GL-207 Super Hercules, for delivery in early 1962, and that Slick Airways was to receive six later in the year. They were to differ from the C-130B in being 23ft 4in longer, with wingspan increased by 12ft 5in and were to have a maximum take-off gross weight of 204,17lb. However, Pan American and Slick cancelled their orders and, since then, all commercial versions of the C-130 have been straightforward developments of

➤

C-130A N133HP (formerly 57-0482) fire-bomber of Hawkins & Powers at Greybull, Wyoming, in August 1989. C-130s that are used on forest fire-control missions are fitted with six 500 US gallon (1,893 litre) pressurised air tanks, dual nozzles and spraying gear located on the main ramp. Each aircraft can dump 3,000 US gallons (11,356 litres) of spray cargo. (Author)

▲

the production aircraft. A total of 114 L-100 models have been built. They differ from the military Hercules in that the underwing fuel tanks have been omitted, and most military equipment removed, although the aircraft can be fitted with retractable combination wheel-skis. The L-100 demonstrator (382-3946 N1130E) flew for the first time on 20/21 April 1964 and remained airborne for twenty-five hours and one minute. All except thirty-six minutes of this time were flown using

L-100, which was acquired by Delta Airlines in August 1966. This aircraft was modified to L-100-20 in December 1968, and sold to Saturn in September 1973. (Lockheed via GMS)

just two of the 4,050eshp Allison 501-D22 engines, the commercial version of the T56. N1130E was subsequently modified to Model 382E/L-100-20, being 'stretched', with a 5ft fuselage plug forward of the wing and a 3.3ft plug aft, to bring the cabin hold volume from 4,500 cubic feet to 5,335 cubic feet. Eight more L-100s were later stretched to become L-100-20 models. The first commercial L-100 operator was Alaska Airlines, which, on 8 March 1965, put into service the Hercules demonstrator,

C-130E 69-6566 at Mildenhall Air Fête in May 1994. (Author)

➤➤

USAF C-130s at the Mildenhall Air Fête in 1998. In 1978 the annual air fête became a two-day event and was a regular fixture in the aviation calendar until 2001. (Author)

on lease from Lockheed. It later leased four more L-100s and purchased one, but by the end of the 1960s had disposed of all of them. Twenty-one production aircraft (Model 382B) were built. The first delivery of L-100, to Continental Air Services, took place on 30 September 1965.

Twenty-seven L-100-20s, including the nine modified from L-100s, have been produced, and the first entered service with Interior Airways in October 1968. Eight L-100-20s were later modified to L-100-30 configuration, and one, an ex-Kuwaiti L-100-20, was modified as the experimental HTTB (High Technology Test Bed) for the C-130J. The L-100-30, the first of which entered service with Saturn Airways, in December 1970, is the main commercial version of the Hercules. Twelve converted L-100s, stretched 15ft, were followed by fifty-three new-build examples. Five L-100-30s, including two configured as a dental clinic, were modified for use in Saudi Arabia as airborne hospitals. In 1992 and 1993 two were demodified to L-100-30s and their hospital equipment removed, and two of the others finished up in Libya. A proposed development and production of the L-400 Twin Hercules, a smaller and lighter version powered by two 4,910eshp Allison 501-D22Ds, and the development of the L-400, were shelved.

In 1991 Lockheed-Martin Aeronautical Systems Company began designing the C-130J. This version is significantly cheaper to operate and support than the C-130H, with substantial improvements in life-cycle costs. In March 1994, when initial cutting of metal began with the fabrication of parts for the first five aircraft, a mock-up unit and two sets of spares, marketing forecasts showed anticipated sales of from 400 to 700 C-130J aircraft in the following ten years. The C-130J development program, funded independently, revealed many technological barriers that had to be surmounted, and it cost Lockheed-Martin at least $400 million in the process. The new state-of-the-art avionics permit a reduction in crew from four to two. The Allison AE-2100D3 two-spool powerplant, with an oil-bath engine starter and new modular gearbox, which replace the earlier T56 engine, is modular and lighter in weight, giving twenty-nine per cent more take-off thrust and fifteen per cent better fuel economy. The Dowty-designed composite R391 scimitar-shaped, six-bladed propeller unit is lighter, has fewer parts and delivers thirteen per cent more thrust. Because the new engine/propeller combination and reduced drag increases range by twenty per cent, there is no real need for external fuel tanks, although the C-130J can carry an additional 18,700lb of fuel in external tanks if required. The carbon-fiber flaps and flap shrouds are manufactured by Shorts. Other innovations include Mk.IV carbon brakes, coupled with an automatic braking feature, and a new anti-skid system, to shorten landing distances. A new modular wheel and integral self-jacking struts greatly reduces

Did you know?

By the mid-1990s there was in active service over sixty of the 231 C-130As built; approximately 130 C-130Bs out of 230 delivered, and of the 491 C-130Es built, more than 310 were in worldwide service with the US armed forces and about ninety others in operational use with armed forces of various other countries.

◄◄
C-130J, the current model of Hercules. The C-130J prototype was rolled out at Marietta, Georgia, on 10 October 1995, and it first flew on 5 April 1996. (Lockheed-Martin)

◄
Close up of the Dowty-designed composite R391 scimitar-bladed propeller unit tested on XV181. (Marshall Aerospace)

the time required to change a wheel, and make it possible to replace tyres at remote sites without ground-support equipment. A new nose-gear strut improves stability so it can taxi more confidently on rough airstrips. An updated electronic system with two new converters provides stable power to all avionics and electronic loads.

C-130J flight dynamics HUD. (Lockheed-Martin)

Cruising at an average of 310 knots, at up to 30,200ft, the 'old' C-130 burns approximately 5,000lb of fuel per hour. The C-130J and C-130J-30 have a maximum internal fuel load of 45,900lb (although the maximum is reduced by slightly over 2,000lb when foam is introduced into the tanks). Lockheed estimates the range of the C-130J to be about 3,000 nautical miles without external tanks. The C-130J-30's added length adds 3,729lb to the aircraft's empty weight, and reduces payload by the same amount. However, the stretched C-130J can carry two additional pallets, as compared to the C-130J, and ninety-two paratroops, as opposed to sixty-four for the standard C-130J.

A new fuel system has a single cross-ship manifold, with half as many fuel-control valves. Lockheed has relocated the in-flight refuelling probe from the centre of the fuselage to the left side, over the pilot's head, to make it easier for the co-pilot when in-flight refuelling is being performed.

The cockpit is still approached via a near-vertical ladder, and the two crew-rest bunks remain at the rear of the cockpit.

Although the flight engineer and navigator stations have been eliminated, there is provision for a third crewmember to sit behind the centre console, between the two pilots, to monitor the flight, or to operate the aircraft's systems, as required. The superb 'greenhouse' windowing providing unparalleled all-round vision has also been retained (although two in the nose have been blanked off). The galley has been turned through 90° to face into the cockpit instead of over the ladder, as previously. The control yokes, the nose-wheel (steering wheel) and the parking-brake handle have been retained, but the cockpit systems include a digital autopilot, a fully integrated global positioning system, colour weather and ground-mapping radar and a digital map display, plus an advisory caution and warning system that allows for fault detection. Mission effectiveness has been infinitely improved thanks to a mission computer allied to electronically controlled

The flight engineer and navigator stations have been eliminated in the C-130J cockpit, which is equipped with four flat-panel liquid-crystal (LCD) head-down (HDD) colour displays, which present all the information needed to fly the aircraft and make available data and navigation plans, including traffic and ground collision avoidance, Advisory Caution and Warning System (ACAWA) messages and SKE-2000 (Station Keeping Equipment) information. Two flight dynamics holographic head-up (HUD) displays permit both pilots to maintain a constant out-of-the-window view while monitoring all the data necessary to control the aircraft. (Lockheed-Martin)

➤
*C.5 (C-1340J-30)
N130JN/ZH868 of the
RAF. (Lockheed-Martin)*

➤➤
*RAF Hercules heading
south to the Congo in
1998. (MoD)*

Did you know?

From 1962 to May
1975 the Nirou Haval
Shahanshahiye Iran
(Imperial Iranian Air
Force) took delivery
of sixty-four Hercules
aircraft, making it the
third largest user of
the C-130 after the US
and the RAF.

engines and propellers, databus architecture and digital avionics. Engine status is present on one of the four flat-panel, liquid-crystal (LCD), head-down (HDD) colour displays on vertical bars. The Westinghouse AN/ APN-24I weather/navigation radar display presents the primary navigation plan, showing the aircraft proceeding along a flight-plan course on a map overlay. Eight different navigational tasks are carried out

*C-5 (C-130J-30)
ZH889 on a sortie over
the Gloucestershire
countryside, going via
the Severn Bridge and
Weston-super-Mare
in September 2001.
(Author)*

C.4 (C-130J) 882 at IWM Duxford in October 2005. The C-130J-30 is the stretched version, which in RAF service is known as the C.5. (Author)

automatically. A second display presents Advisory Caution and Warning System (ACAWA) messages and SKE-2000 (Station Keeping Equipment) information. The fourth display presents all information necessary to fly the aircraft. Two flight dynamic holographic head-up (HUD) displays permit both pilots to maintain a constant tour-of-the-window view while monitoring all the data necessary to control the aircraft. As a

C.4 (C-130J) 882 at IWM Duxford in October 2005. The C-130J-30 is the stretched version, which in RAF service is known as the C.5. (Author)

fail-safe there are two mission computers, although one computer is capable of doing all tasks.

Problems with the liquid-crystal cockpit displays, and the totally unexpected problem of stalling during flight-testing, caused long delays to the C-130J development program, and a consequent lag in production aircraft delivery. N130JA/ ZH865, the C-130J prototype, which was rolled out at Marietta on 18 October 1995, flew for the first time on 5 April 1996.

The largest operator of the new model is the USAF, though it is also operated extensively by the US ANG and USCG. The RAF have received twenty-five C-130J-30/C-4 and C-130J/C.5 aircraft, while the Danish, Italian, Australian, Norwegian and New Zealand Air Forces also have examples in their transport fleets.

SPECIFICATIONS

C-130E Hercules

Powerplant: Four Allison T56-A-7 turboprops, each rated at 4,050eshp

Weights: Operating 73,563lb (33,368kg); maximum take-off 15,000lb (70,308kg); maximum payload 45,5791b (20,674kg)

Dimensions: Span 132ft 7in (40.41m); length 97ft 9in (29.79m); height 38ft 3in (11.66m); wing area 1,745sq ft (162.12sq m)

Performance: Maximum speed 384mph (618km/h); cruising speed 368mph (592km/h); rate of climb 1,830ft/min (558m/min); ceiling 23,000ft (7,010m); take-off to 50ft 5,580ft (1,700m); landing at 130,000lb from 50ft 3,750ft (1,143m); range with maximum payload and reserves 2,420 miles (3,895km); range with maximum fuel 4,700 miles (7,560km)

C-130H Hercules

Powerplant: Four Allison T56-A-15 turboprops, each rated at 4,508eshp

Weights: Operating 76,5051b (34,702kg); maximum take-off 155,000lb (70,308kg); maximum payload 42,637lb (19,340kg)

Dimensions: Span 132ft 7in (40.41m); length 97ft 9in (29.79m); height 38ft 3in (11.66m); wing area 1,745sq ft (162.12sq m)

Performance: Maximum speed 385mph (620km/h); long-range cruising speed 332mph (535km/h); rate of climb 1,900ft/min (579m/min); ceiling at 130,00lb 33,000ft (10,060m); take-off to 50ft 5,160ft (l,573m); landing at 100,000lb from 50ft 2,400ft (731m); range with maximum payload and reserves 2,356 miles (3,791km); range with maximum fuel 4,894 miles (7,876km)

C-130J HERCULES

Powerplant: Four Allison AE2100D3 turboprops, each rated at 4,591eshp

Weights: Operating 79,090lb (35,875kg); maximum take-off 155,000lb (70,308kg); maximum payload 41,043lb (18,617kg)

Dimensions: Span 132ft 7in (40.41m); length 97ft 9in (29.79m); height 38ft 3in (11.66m); wing area 1,745sq ft (162.12sq m)

Performance: Cruising speed 365mph (586km/h); rate of climb 2,234ft/min (681m/min); ceiling at 100,00lb, 40,000ft (12,103m); range with maximum payload 2,700 miles (4,563km); range with maximum fuel 4,700 miles (7,562km)

Did you know?
Lockheed-Martin began designing the C-130J in 1991, and by January 1998 almost fifty British firms were supporting the C-130J project on a risk-sharing basis, with more than £470 million of orders having been placed in the UK.

MILESTONES

January 1951: Lockheed reopens Plant 6, a government-built factory at the vast seventy-six-acre site at Marietta, fifteen miles from Atlanta.

2 February 1951: USAF issues a Request for Proposals (RFP) to Boeing, Douglas, Fairchild and Lockheed for a medium-size transport complying with a specially prepared General Operational Requirement (GOR).

10 February 1951: First seven C-130As ordered.

March 1951: C-130H-LM (Model 382C) first delivered to the RNZAF.

April 1951: Lockheed L-206 proposal submitted.

7 April 1951: C-130A-LM (53-3129) flown for first time.

2 July 1951: Lockheed L-206 declared the winner.

23 August 1951: second YC-130 prototype (1002/53-3397) flies at the Lockheed air terminal.

19 September 1951: Lockheed awarded a contract for two YC-130 (Model 82) prototype/service-test aircraft, to be built at Burbank, and Pentagon issues a letter contract for seven production aircraft.

December 1951: Contract issued for 127 C-130Bs (Model 282) for Tactical Air Command.

1951: Lockheed announces that Pan American Airways have ordered twelve GE-207 Super Hercules for delivery in early 1962.

10 March 1954: First production C-130A-LM (53-3129) rolled out at Marietta.

April 1954 Pentagon orders a further twenty C-130As.

August 1955: Fourth contract issued for eighty-four Hercules.

June 1956: Two C-130As delivered to USAF Air Proving Ground Command at Eglin AFB.

9 December 1956: First operational C-130s for the USAF delivered.

1960: GL-307 version with 6,445eshp Rolls-Royce Tynes and a gross weight of 230,000lb proposed.

April 1962: Deliveries of the first of 389 C-130Es for Military Airlift Command (MAC) begin.

20/21 April 1964: L-100 demonstrator (382-3946 N1130E) flies for the first time.

April 1965: Hercules C.Mk.1 enters service with 2 OCU at Thorney Island.

8 March 1965: Alaska Airlines becomes first commercial L-100 operator, putting Hercules demonstrator, on lease from Lockheed, into service.

8-12 March 1965: C-130s deploy a Marine battalion landing team from Okinawa to Da Nang, South Vietnam.

4-7 May 1965: C-130s carry the US Army's 173rd Airborne Brigade to South Vietnam in 140 lifts.

19 October 1966: C-130K flies for the first time.

February 1968: A total of ninety-six C-130s are stationed in Vietnam.

4 October 1968: L-100-20 certificated.

April 1970: Decision taken to convert two C-130Es to AC-130E prototype gunships.

July-November 1972: Hercules flies 708,087 sorties in Vietnam.

24 April 1980: Joint USAF/USMC attempt to rescue US hostages in Iran using Hercules and Navy helicopters ends in disaster at 'Desert One'.

16 to 28 August 1990: Fifteen C-130Es of Military Aircraft Command's become the first European-based USAF aircraft deployed to South-West Asia for Desert Shield.

15 January 1991: Operation Desert Storm begins. By the time the cease-fire comes into effect on 3 March, MAC C-130 transports will have, since 10 August 1990, flown 46,500 sorties and moved more than 209,000 personnel and 300,000 tons of supplies within the theatre.

18 October 1995: C-130J (RAF Hercules C.4/ZH865) prototype rolled out at Lockheed-Marietta.

5 April 1996: C-130J flies for first time.